THE American Regional COOK BOOK

by Barbara Grunes

ideals®

Ideals Publishing Corp.
Nashville, Tennessee

Contents

Director of Publishing Patricia A. Pingry
Cookbook Editor Teri Mitchell
Copy Editor Susan DuBois
Art Director Jennifer Rundberg
Staff Artist David Lenz

ISBN 0-8249-3054-1
Copyright © MCMLXXXV by Ideals Publishing Corporation
All rights reserved.
Printed and bound in the United States of America.

Published by Ideals Publishing Corporation
P.O. Box 141000
Nashville, Tennessee 37214-1000

Boston Cream Pie, page 9

Cover Photo: New England Boiled Dinner, page 8; Cornish Pasties, page 40; Cherry Pie, page 61

New England

Boston Clam Chowder
Makes 6 Servings

5 slices bacon, cut into ½-inch pieces
1 large onion, thinly sliced
2½ pounds littleneck clams
4 large potatoes, boiled and diced
1 quart milk
2 cups whipping cream
Salt and pepper
4 tablespoons butter
Crackers

Fry bacon pieces in a large heavy skillet; remove bacon and reserve. Reheat drippings; sauté onion until soft, stirring occasionally. Remove and reserve onion. Steam clams in a covered kettle filled to a ¾-inch depth with water. Steam for 5 to 7 minutes. Strain and reserve the clam juice. Discard any unopened clams. Remove clams from shells; discard shells. Chop clams; set aside. Combine potatoes, bacon, onion, clam juice, and enough water to cover in a large saucepan. Bring chowder to a boil over medium heat; reduce heat and simmer for 4 to 5 minutes. Add milk and cream; season with salt and pepper to taste. Stir in clams and butter; simmer 5 minutes or until butter melts. Serve with crackers.

Boston Baked Beans
Makes 6 to 8 servings

1 pound dried pea beans
2 cups water
1 teaspoon dry mustard
½ teaspoon powdered ginger
2 large onions, thinly sliced
Salt
¼ cup firmly packed dark brown sugar
¼ cup dark molasses
¼ pound salt pork, cut into ½-inch pieces

Wash beans carefully and remove any foreign particles. Soak beans overnight in a large pot with enough water to cover. Add 2 cups water, mustard, ginger, and onion. Cover and cook over medium heat for 50 minutes to 1 hour or until beans are tender. Add salt to taste. Transfer beans to a bean pot or ovenproof casserole; stir in brown sugar and molasses. Place salt pork on top of beans. Cover and bake at 250° for 5 to 6 hours, stirring occasionally. Add water during baking so the beans remain covered with liquid. Serve warm.

Boiled Potatoes
Makes 6 servings

12 small new Maine potatoes, washed and skin intact
3 tablespoons butter
4 tablespoons minced fresh parsley

Place potatoes in a large pot with salted water to a depth of 1 inch; bring to a boil. Cover pan and steam potatoes over high heat for 15 to 20 minutes or until potatoes are tender. Place potatoes in a shallow serving dish and toss with butter and parsley. Serve hot.

Harvard Beets

Makes 6 servings

6 large beets, cooked, peeled, and sliced
2 onions, thinly sliced
½ cup sugar
4 tablespoons cornstarch combined with 3 tablespoons melted butter
4 tablespoons wine vinegar
Grated orange peel

Combine beets and onion in a heavy saucepan; set aside. Combine all remaining ingredients except orange peel in a small bowl and add to beets; mix well. Bring mixture to a boil over medium heat; reduce heat to simmer and continue cooking, stirring occasionally, until the mixture thickens slightly. Arrange beets in a deep serving dish and garnish with orange peel.

Boiled Maine Lobster

Makes 2 servings

2 tablespoons salt
2 live lobsters (1½ pounds each)
Melted butter

Add salt to a large pot of rapidly boiling water. Add lobsters, head first. Cover pot and continue cooking over high heat for 5 to 7 minutes. Lobsters will be bright red. Drain lobsters; crack claws. Slit lobster; remove and discard the intestinal vein, liver, and stomach. Serve lobsters hot with melted butter.

Fried Clams with Tartar Sauce

Makes 4 servings

5 dozen clams, shucked
3 eggs, well beaten
2 cups bread crumbs
Vegetable oil
Tartar Sauce (see recipe below)

Rinse clams well under cold running water; pat dry with paper towels. Dip clams in egg; roll in bread crumbs. Pour oil into a saucepan to a depth of 2 inches; heat to 375°. Fry clams 1 cup at a time until golden brown; drain on paper towels. Continue frying clams until all are cooked. Serve hot with Tartar Sauce.

Tartar Sauce

Makes ¾ cup sauce

½ cup mayonnaise
2 tablespoons chopped sweet pickles
2 tablespoons minced onion
2 tablespoons chopped fresh parsley
2 teaspoons capers

Combine all ingredients in a small bowl. Cover and refrigerate until ready to serve.

Boston Brown Bread

Makes 1 loaf or 2 small loaves

1 egg, slightly beaten
3 tablespoons sugar
1 cup dark molasses
¾ cup buttermilk
½ teaspoon salt
1 cup whole-wheat flour
1 cup flour
¾ teaspoon baking soda
¾ teaspoon baking powder
½ cup raisins

Preheat oven to 350°. Grease a clean 2-pound coffee can or two 1-pound cans. Combine egg, sugar, molasses, and buttermilk in a deep mixing bowl. Add salt, flour, baking soda, and baking powder; mix well. Gently stir in raisins. Pour batter into prepared can. Bake for 40 to 50 minutes or until cake tester inserted in center comes out clean.

Yankee Pot Roast

Makes 5 to 6 servings

2½ pounds beef chuck roast
3 tablespoons flour
3 tablespoons bacon
  drippings
1 cup beef stock
¾ cup tomato sauce
½ teaspoon salt
¼ teaspoon freshly ground
  pepper
6 potatoes, quartered
5 stalks celery, cut into
  thirds
4 large carrots, quartered
3 large onions, quartered
2 green peppers, quartered
1 teaspoon Worcestershire
  sauce

Dust meat with flour. Heat bacon drippings in a Dutch oven; brown meat on all sides over medium heat. Stir in beef stock and tomato sauce; add remaining ingredients. Cover; reduce heat to simmer. Simmer for 2 hours or until meat is tender. Stir occasionally, adding liquid as necessary. Taste and adjust seasonings if needed. Serve hot.

Backyard Clambake

Makes 6 servings

1 bushel seaweed, washed,
  still wet
6 live lobsters (1 pound
  each)
6 ears corn in the husk
3 pounds clams
  Melted butter

Use an outdoor fireplace or open barbecue pit for convenience. In the bottom of a very large, heavy kettle, place a layer of wet seaweed. Kill lobsters by severing vein at the base of the neck; arrange them over the seaweed. Add another layer of seaweed; top with corn in the husk. Add a third layer of seaweed; top with clams and a final layer of seaweed. Cover tightly and cook over hot fire for 2 hours or until clams are cooked. Discard any unopened clams. Serve clams first, then corn; serve the cooked lobster last. Serve with melted butter.

Boston Brown Bread, this page

New England Boiled Dinner

Makes 6 to 8 servings

3½ to 4 pounds corned beef
1 head cabbage, cut into eighths
6 carrots, cut into thirds
2 onions, quartered
½ pound brussels sprouts
8 small new potatoes, halved
2 large turnips, cut into eighths

Cover corned beef with cold water and set aside for 20 minutes; drain. Place meat in a large pot; add enough water to cover meat. Bring to a boil; reduce heat and simmer, covered, for 2½ hours. Add remaining ingredients and continue cooking for 1 hour or until meat and vegetables are fork-tender. Slice meat and place on serving platter; garnish with drained vegetables.

Parker House Rolls

Makes 12 rolls

½ teaspoon salt
2 teaspoons sugar
2 tablespoons butter, melted
1 cup scalded milk
1 package active dry yeast
3½ cups flour

Stir salt, sugar, and melted butter into the milk; set aside and cool to lukewarm. Dissolve yeast in 5 tablespoons warm (105° to 115°) water; set aside in a draft-free area for 5 minutes. Combine yeast with milk mixture; stir in ⅓ of the flour. Knead in remaining flour. Place in a lightly greased bowl, turning once to grease top. Place in a draft-free area. Let rise, covered, for 1¼ hours or until doubled in bulk. Punch dough down; roll out and cut into circles. Using the floured handle of a wooden spoon make a crease in middle of each roll. Fold over and press edges together gently. Let rolls rise for 30 minutes. Preheat oven to 375°. Bake for 12 to 15 minutes or until rolls are golden brown. Cool on wire rack.

Indian Pudding

Makes 6 servings

¼ cup cornmeal
2 cups milk, heated
3 tablespoons butter
¼ teaspoon salt
¾ cup dark molasses
½ teaspoon ginger
½ teaspoon cinnamon
1½ cups milk, divided
Vanilla ice cream

Preheat oven to 350°. Combine cornmeal with milk in the top of a double boiler. Place over boiling water; bring mixture to a boil over medium heat. Whisk in butter, salt, molasses, and spices. Continue cooking, stirring often, for 10 minutes, or until mixture thickens. Pour into a well-greased 2-quart baking dish. Bake pudding uncovered for 25 minutes. Stir in ½ cup milk. Reduce heat to 250°; bake for 1 hour. Pour remaining milk over top of pudding; bake for 2 hours longer. Serve warm with vanilla ice cream.

Boston Cream Pie

Makes 6 to 8 servings

Cake

6 tablespoons butter
¾ cup sugar
2 eggs, slightly beaten
1 teaspoon vanilla
1½ cups cake flour
2 teaspoons baking powder
¼ teaspoon salt
½ cup milk

Preheat oven to 375°. Grease two 9-inch cake pans; set aside. Cream butter and sugar in a mixing bowl until light; blend in eggs and vanilla. Combine flour, baking powder, and salt in a small bowl. Slowly sprinkle flour mixture over butter, alternately adding flour and milk. Pour batter into pans; bake for 15 minutes or until cake tester inserted in center comes out clean. Cool on rack. Prepare filling.

Filling

1 cup scalded milk, cooled
½ cup sugar
2 tablespoons cornstarch *or* flour
3 eggs, slightly beaten
1 teaspoon vanilla

Pour milk into saucepan; add sugar. Cook over medium heat until sugar has dissolved, stirring constantly. In a small bowl, whisk cornstarch into eggs until smooth. Add 2 tablespoons of milk mixture to eggs; add eggs to milk mixture, whisking until blended. Continue cooking over low heat until mixture thickens slightly. Remove from heat; stir in vanilla. Cool to room temperature. Prepare icing.

Chocolate Icing

3 ounces semi-sweet chocolate
2 tablespoons butter
¼ cup milk *or* cream
½ cup powdered sugar
½ teaspoon vanilla

Melt chocolate and butter in top of double boiler over warm water. Remove from heat and blend in milk. Beat in powdered sugar until smooth. Add vanilla; mix well.

To Assemble: Remove cake layers from pan. Place 1 layer bottom-side up. Spread custard carefully over top. Gently adjust second layer top-side up over custard. Drizzle icing over top of cake using a circular motion on the edge so that the icing will flow down the sides of the cake. Chill cake until ready to serve.

New York–Pennsylvania

Baked Apples
Makes 6 servings

6 large baking apples, cored and top 1½ inches peeled
½ cup golden raisins
¼ cup firmly packed dark brown sugar
½ teaspoon cinnamon
3 tablespoons butter, cut into small chunks

Preheat over to 400°. Arrange apples in a large pie plate. Mix together raisins, sugar, and cinnamon in a small bowl. Stuff apples with filling; dot tops with butter. Place apples in pie plate; pour ½ cup of water in bottom of plate. Bake for 30 to 40 minutes; remove from oven. Place on individual dessert dishes.

Bagels
Makes 18 bagels

1 package active dry yeast
1 tablespoon sugar
1 teaspoon salt
4 cups flour

Gently stir yeast in a mixing bowl with 1½ cups warm (105° to 115°) water. Set aside in a draft-free area for 5 minutes. Mix in sugar, salt, and just enough flour to make a soft dough. On a lightly floured board, knead dough until it is smooth and elastic, adding the remaining flour as needed. Place dough in a greased bowl; turn once. Cover; let stand in a warm, draft-free area for 15 minutes; punch dough down. Divide dough into 18 pieces. Roll each piece gently on floured board to form a ½-inch thick and 7-inch long rope. Moisten ends and press together to form bagels. Arrange bagels on floured cookie sheets. Let stand loosely covered with a towel for 20 minutes. Preheat oven to 375°. Fill a large, heavy skillet with water and bring to a boil over medium heat. Reduce heat to simmer; place 4 bagels in skillet. Simmer, uncovered, for 3 minutes. Turn bagels over; simmer for 3 to 4 minutes more. Drain on paper towels. Repeat with remaining bagels. Place bagels on ungreased cookie sheets; bake for 25 to 30 minutes or until golden brown. Cool on wire rack.

Raisin-Bran Muffins
Makes 12 muffins

1¼ cups flour
2 cups bran flakes
¼ teaspoon salt
1 teaspoon baking soda
1 egg, well beaten
1¼ cups milk
¼ cup dark molasses
1 cup dark raisins

Preheat oven to 400°; grease muffin tin. Combine dry ingredients in a large, deep mixing bowl. Add egg, milk, and molasses; gently mix ingredients together. Add raisins; stir just to blend. Fill muffin cups ⅔ full. Bake for 25 minutes; remove from oven and cool on rack.

Baked Apples, this page

Pepper Pot Soup
Makes 6 to 8 servings

½ pound tripe, cut into ½-
  inch pieces
2 meaty veal knuckles *or*
  shank bones
  Salt and pepper
  Dried red pepper flakes
3 tablespoons butter
1 large onion, thinly sliced
1 large green pepper,
  chopped
4 large potatoes, cubed
2 bay leaves

Place tripe, veal knuckles, and water to cover in a large soup pot. Bring to a boil over medium heat; reduce heat to simmer. Add salt, pepper, and red pepper flakes to taste. Simmer for 2 hours; skim foam off as needed. Strain soup stock; reserve tripe. Remove meat from veal bones; reserve. Return stock to pot. Heat butter in a heavy skillet; sauté onion and pepper until tender. Add to stock along with potatoes, veal meat, tripe, and bay leaves. Bring soup to a boil; reduce heat to simmer. Continue cooking, partially covered, for 45 minutes. Adjust seasonings.

Waldorf Salad
Makes 6 servings

6 Red Delicious apples,
  cored and diced (leave
  peel intact)
1 tablespoon sugar
  Juice of ½ large lemon
3 stalks celery, diced
1 cup coarsely chopped
  pecans
½ cup mayonnaise
¼ cup heavy cream, chilled
  and whipped
6 whole lettuce leaves

Toss apples with sugar and lemon juice in a deep bowl. Mix in celery and nuts. Blend mayonnaise and whipped cream in a small bowl; combine with celery mixture. Arrange lettuce on chilled salad plates. Mound salad in center of lettuce leaves.

Cole Slaw
Makes 8 servings

1 large head cabbage,
  shredded
1 cup shredded red cabbage
1 large carrot, grated
1 medium onion, diced
3 tablespoons wine vinegar
1 tablespoon sugar
¾ cup mayonnaise
  Salt, pepper, and garlic
  powder

Toss cabbage, carrot, and onion in a large mixing bowl. Combine vinegar, sugar, and mayonnaise in a small bowl. Pour mayonnaise mixture over vegetables; toss. Season with salt, pepper, and garlic powder to taste. Cover and refrigerate for 2 hours before serving.

Seafood Newburg
Makes 6 servings

5 tablespoons butter
2 tablespoons flour *or* cornstarch
1 pint half-and-half *or* cream
¼ teaspoon salt
⅛ teaspoon white pepper
⅛ teaspoon nutmeg
2 egg yolks, well beaten
3 cups cooked seafood, flaked *or* cut into ¾-inch pieces
3 tablespoons dry sherry, optional
6 puff pastry shells, baked

Melt butter in a small saucepan over medium heat. Whisk in flour and cook for 2 to 3 minutes until flour is absorbed. Blend in half-and-half, salt, pepper, and nutmeg, and cook until thickened, stirring often. Remove sauce from heat. Place egg yolks in a small bowl and whisk in ¼ cup of sauce. Pour the egg mixture into the sauce, whisking constantly. Mix in seafood and simmer until just warm. Stir in sherry. Ladle Seafood Newburg into and around hot puff pastry shells.

Stuffed Clams
Makes 6 servings

2 to 2¼ pounds littleneck clams, scrubbed
5 to 6 tablespoons butter
2 cloves garlic, minced
6 green onions, minced
4 tablespoons minced parsley
1 cup cracker crumbs
   Salt and pepper
   Grated Parmesan cheese

Arrange clams in a large pot; add water to a depth of 1 inch. Cover tightly and bring to a boil; continue cooking for 7 minutes. Discard any unopened shells. Drain clams; reserve liquid. Chop clams, reserving shells. Preheat oven to 400°. Melt butter in a large heavy skillet; sauté garlic and onion until soft, stirring occasionally. Stir in parsley, crumbs, and clams; season to taste with salt and pepper. Add enough clam juice to slightly moisten mixture; mound in reserved clam shells. Arrange clams on a cookie sheet. Sprinkle with cheese. Bake for 5 to 6 minutes or until hot. Serve immediately.

Scrapple
Makes 6 to 8 servings

2 cups cornmeal
1½ pounds cooked pork, chopped
½ teaspoon salt
¼ teaspoon pepper
1 onion, minced
   Flour
4 tablespoons butter

Bring 2 quarts water to a boil; slowly add cornmeal and cook until thick, stirring constantly. Add pork, seasonings, and onion; continue cooking for 10 minutes. Rinse a shallow oblong pan with cold water; pour mixture into pan. Refrigerate overnight. Cut scrapple into slices; dip in flour. Heat butter in heavy skillet. Fry scrapple on both sides until golden brown.

New York Cheesecake

Makes 10 to 12 servings

Butter
2 8-ounce packages cream cheese, softened
2 8-ounce cartons cream-style cottage cheese
1½ cups sugar
5 eggs
3 tablespoons cornstarch
1½ tablespoons freshly squeezed lemon juice
1 tablespoon vanilla
¼ stick butter, melted and cooled
2 8-ounce cartons sour cream
1 21-ounce can blueberry pie filling

Preheat oven to 325°. Lightly butter a 9-inch springform pan. Blend cream cheese and cottage cheese in a large bowl until smooth. Add sugar and eggs; beat for about 10 minutes or until light and fluffy. Mix in all remaining ingredients except pie filling. Mix until completely blended. Pour filling into prepared pan. Bake for 1 hour and 10 minutes, or until cake is firm. Turn off oven. Leave cake in oven for 2 hours with door closed. Remove cake from oven; cool completely. Refrigerate at least 6 hours before serving. When ready to serve, run a spatula around sides of pan to loosen cake; remove from pan. Top with blueberry pie filling.

Popovers

8 popovers

2 cups flour
¼ teaspoon salt
2 cups milk
2 eggs, slightly beaten
2 tablespoons butter, melted

Preheat oven to 450°; place popover pans in oven. Sift flour and salt together. Pour eggs into a large mixing bowl; alternately add flour and milk to eggs, stirring to blend. Mix in melted butter. Beat with an electric mixer until batter is smooth. Fill *hot* (preheated) popover pans ⅔ full with batter. Place pan immediately in hot oven and bake for 30 minutes. Reduce temperature to 350° and continue baking for 15 minutes. Serve immediately with butter.

Shoo-Fly Pie

Makes 6 to 8 servings

1½ cups flour
¾ cup firmly packed light brown sugar
½ teaspoon cinnamon
¼ teaspoon nutmeg
¼ teaspoon salt
6 tablespoons butter at room temperature, cut into ½-inch pieces
½ cup dark molasses
½ teaspoon baking soda
1 9-inch pie crust, unbaked
Whipped cream *or* vanilla ice cream

Combine first 6 ingredients in a large mixing bowl; mix well. Set crumb topping mixture aside. Preheat oven to 375°. Place molasses in a small bowl; stir in baking soda. Add ½ cup boiling water. Add 1¾ cups topping; blend into molasses mixture. Pour filling into unbaked pie crust. Sprinkle remaining crumb topping over pie. Bake pie for 45 minutes or until golden brown. Serve warm with whipped cream or vanilla ice cream.

New York Cheesecake, this page

South Atlantic Coast

Peanut Soup

Makes 6 servings

3 tablespoons butter
1 onion, minced
3 stalks celery, chopped
3½ cups chicken stock
1¼ cups chunk-style peanut butter
½ teaspoon honey
1 pint half-and-half
½ cup chopped peanuts

Heat butter in a medium saucepan; sauté onion and celery until tender, stirring often. Add chicken stock and peanut butter; stir until smooth. Turn heat to low; simmer for 10 minutes. Add honey and half-and-half; continue heating until soup is hot. Serve garnished with chopped peanuts.

She-Crab Soup

Makes 6 servings

2 tablespoons butter
2 teaspoons flour
1 pint milk
1 pint heavy cream
¼ teaspoon each mace, salt, and white pepper
2 cups crab meat
2 eggs, slightly beaten
1 teaspoon grated lemon peel
6 tablespoons dry sherry

Melt butter in double boiler over simmering water. Whisk in flour for 2 to 3 minutes or until absorbed. Blend in milk, cream, and seasonings; add crab meat. Add 2 tablespoons soup to eggs; mix. Add eggs and grated lemon peel to soup. Simmer for 10 minutes, stirring occasionally. Pour 1 tablespoon sherry in each bowl. Fill with warm soup; serve.

Crab Cakes

Makes 4 to 6 servings

1 pound Dungeness crab meat, drained, flaked, and cartilage removed
2 eggs, slightly beaten
1 onion, minced
1 tablespoon prepared mustard
1 tablespoon mayonnaise
½ teaspoon salt
1 cup mashed potatoes
Peanut oil

Combine all ingredients except oil in a deep bowl. Shape into croquettes. Pour 2 inches of oil into a heavy skillet; heat to 375°. Slide croquettes, 1 at a time, into the oil. Fry in batches of 3 until golden brown on all sides. Drain on paper towels. Serve hot.

Virginia Baked Ham with Mustard Sauce

Makes 8 servings

1 fully cooked 9 to 10 pound ham at room temperature
Whole cloves
Mustard Sauce (see recipe below)

Preheat oven to 325°. Arrange ham on rack in roasting pan, fat side up. Place a meat thermometer in the thickest part of ham. Pour ¾ cup water in bottom of pan to prevent smoking. Bake ham for 1 hour. Remove from oven and use a sharp knife to score a diamond pattern in ham. Insert a whole clove at points of the pattern and continue baking for ½ hour or until internal temperature of 140° is reached. Allow ham to stand for 15 minutes before slicing. Serve ham with Mustard Sauce.

Mustard Sauce

Makes about 1½ cups

2 hard-boiled egg yolks, minced
¼ cup prepared mustard
2 tablespoons Dijon-style mustard
¼ teaspoon salt
1 green onion, minced
2 stalks celery, minced
3 teaspoons tarragon vinegar
½ cup vegetable or olive oil
¼ cup heavy cream

Combine egg yolks, mustard, salt, onion, and celery in a small bowl. Whisk in vinegar. Whisk in oil in a slow steady stream; continue whisking until thickened. Stir in cream; adjust seasonings. Place in a covered container; chill until ready to serve.

Fried Soft-Shell Crabs with Garlic Butter

Makes 6 servings

¾ cup milk
1 egg, slightly beaten
6 soft-shell crabs, cleaned
¼ teaspoon salt
1½ cups flour
Peanut oil
½ cup butter
2 cloves garlic, minced

Combine milk and egg in a large bowl. Sprinkle crabs with salt and place in milk for 10 minutes, turning occasionally. Roll crabs in flour; shake to remove excess. Pour enough oil to cover crabs into a large heavy skillet; heat to 375°. Slide crabs gently into hot oil. Fry crabs for 4 to 5 minutes or until golden brown. Drain on paper towels. Melt butter in a small saucepan; sauté garlic until it begins to brown. Arrange crabs on serving platter and drizzle with garlic butter; serve.

Deviled Crab

Makes 6 servings

5 tablespoons butter
4 tablespoons flour
　Salt, pepper, and paprika
1 pint heavy cream
½ teaspoon dry mustard
1 tablespoon minced capers
2 cups freshly cooked
　Dungeness crab meat,
　drained, flaked, and
　cartilage removed
3 stalks celery, sliced
1 hard-boiled egg, diced
1 cup coarse cracker crumbs

Preheat oven to 350°. Melt butter in a medium saucepan. Add flour and whisk over medium-low heat until flour is absorbed. Stir in salt, pepper, and paprika to taste. Whisk in heavy cream and mustard and continue cooking until sauce thickens. Add remaining ingredients and mix well. Fill buttered ramekins, shells, or 1-quart casserole. Bake for 20 minutes. Serve immediately.

Hopping John

Makes 6 to 8 servings

1 cup dried black-eyed peas
4 cups boiling water, divided
¼ cup bacon drippings
2 onions, thinly sliced
2 stalks celery, diced
1 bay leaf
1 teaspoon salt
¼ teaspoon pepper
½ cup raw rice

Combine peas and 2 cups boiling water in a medium saucepan. Cover and allow to stand for 2 hours. Heat bacon drippings in a large heavy skillet over medium heat. Sauté onion and celery until tender, stirring occasionally. Add vegetables, bay leaf, salt, and pepper to peas. Add remaining 2 cups boiling water. Bring to a boil, cover and simmer for 1 hour or until peas are almost tender. Discard bay leaf; stir in rice. Cover and simmer until rice is cooked. Serve hot.

Key Lime Pie

Makes 6 servings

1 12-ounce can sweetened
　condensed milk
4 egg yolks
　Freshly squeezed juice
　from 3 limes
　Green food coloring,
　optional
1 9-inch pie crust, baked and
　cooled
　Halved lime slices

Combine condensed milk and egg yolks in a deep mixing bowl. Slowly add lime juice; mix well. Add green food coloring if desired. Pour mixture into prepared crust and refrigerate for 3 hours or until pie is firm. Garnish with lime slices.

Key Lime Pie, this page

Candied Sweet Potatoes

Makes 6 to 8 servings

6 tablespoons butter
¼ cup firmly packed dark
  brown sugar
3 tablespoons freshly
  squeezed orange juice
¼ teaspoon cinnamon
6 large sweet potatoes,
  boiled, cooled, and sliced

Melt butter in a large heavy skillet. Stir in sugar, orange juice, and cinnamon. Continue cooking over medium heat until mixture begins to boil. Add potatoes, being careful not to break them. Turn potatoes to coat with brown sugar glaze. Cook for 10 to 15 minutes. Serve hot.

Chess Pie

Makes 2 pies

4 eggs, beaten
2 cups sugar
½ stick butter, cut into ½-inch
  pieces
4 tablespoons heavy cream
¼ teaspoon vanilla
2 9-inch pie crusts

Preheat oven to 375°. Combine all ingredients in a deep bowl. Pour mixture into prepared pie crusts. Bake for 30 minutes or until pie tester inserted in center comes out clean. Cool and serve.

Lady Baltimore Cake

Makes 8 servings

½ cup butter at room
  temperature, cut into ½-
  inch pieces
1 cup sugar
2½ cups cake flour
2½ teaspoons baking powder
¼ teaspoon salt
1 cup milk
1 teaspoon vanilla
4 egg whites, beaten stiff
  Frosting

Preheat oven to 375°. Grease two 8-inch layer cake pans. Cream butter and sugar until light and fluffy. Mix flour, baking powder, and salt in a medium bowl; alternately add flour and milk to butter mixture. Add vanilla to batter, and fold in egg whites. Pour batter into prepared pans; smooth top with spatula. Bake for 20 minutes or until cake tester inserted in center comes out clean. Cool on wire rack. Prepare frosting.

Frosting

2 cups sugar
2 egg whites, beaten stiff
  with ¼ teaspoon cream of
  tartar
1 teaspoon vanilla
1 cup golden raisins and 1
  cup chopped walnuts,
  soaked in ½ cup dry
  sherry overnight

Combine sugar and ½ cup water in a small saucepan; bring to a boil over medium heat, stirring often, until sugar dissolves. In a slow steady stream pour hot syrup into the egg whites while beating. Add vanilla; continue beating until smooth and fluffy. Mix in raisins and walnuts. Frost cake layers immediately.

Banana Ice Cream
Makes 1 quart ice cream

2 eggs
1 cup sugar
¼ teaspoon salt
1 teaspoon vanilla
1 13-ounce can evaporated
  milk
1 pint heavy cream
2 cups mashed ripe bananas

Beat eggs in large bowl with electric mixer until light. Add sugar and salt; continue beating until fluffy. Add vanilla, evaporated milk, cream, and bananas. Process in ice cream maker according to manufacturer's directions or freeze in a shallow tray, purée, and refreeze.

Ambrosia
Makes 5 to 6 servings

6 large oranges, peeled,
  seeded, sectioned, and
  membrane removed
6 bananas, sliced
1 cup freshly grated coconut
  Sugar

Arrange 1 layer of oranges in a serving bowl. Cover with a layer of banana slices; sprinkle with ⅓ cup coconut and sugar to taste. Continue until all fruit is used; end with coconut layer. Cover and chill until ready to serve.

Orange Meringue Pie
Makes 6 to 8 servings

¾ cup sugar
6 tablespoons cornstarch
¼ teaspoon salt
1¼ cups milk
½ cup cream
4 eggs, separated
1 cup freshly squeezed
  orange juice
  Juice of 1 freshly
  squeezed lemon
6 tablespoons sugar
1 9-inch pie crust, baked and
  cooled

Combine sugar, cornstarch and salt in a medium saucepan. Stir in milk and cream; simmer, stirring often, until mixture thickens. Beat egg yolks in a small bowl until light. Add 2 tablespoons of milk mixture to egg yolks. Pour egg yolks in a slow steady stream into milk mixture; stir. Beat in orange juice and lemon juice. Continue cooking over low heat, stirring often, until mixture thickens slightly. Cool filling; pour into pie shell. Refrigerate until pie is firm. Preheat oven to 350°. Beat egg whites until soft peaks form. Beat sugar into egg whites ¼ cup at a time; continue beating until stiff peaks form. Mound meringue over chilled pie. Bake for 10 minutes or until meringue is golden. Chill and serve cold.

The South

Ham Steaks with Red-Eye Gravy

Makes 6 servings

4 tablespoons butter
6 slices ham, ½ inch thick
¼ cup firmly packed dark
  brown sugar
½ cup strong black coffee

Melt butter in a large heavy skillet; sauté ham slices on both sides until lightly browned. Remove ham from pan; set aside. Whisk sugar into pan drippings; cook over low heat, stirring constantly, until sugar melts. Stir in coffee and simmer for 5 minutes. Gravy will be a red-brown color. Serve warm ham slices with gravy.

Crispy Catfish

Makes 6 servings

½ teaspoon salt
¼ teaspoon pepper
1 cup yellow cornmeal
6 large catfish fillets
1 cup evaporated milk
  Peanut oil
½ teaspoon paprika
  Lemon wedges

Combine salt, pepper, and cornmeal in a shallow dish. Dip fish in milk; roll in cornmeal mixture. Pour oil into a large heavy skillet to a depth of 1 inch. Heat oil to 375°. Fry fish a few pieces at a time until golden brown and fish flakes easily with a fork. Drain on paper towels; sprinkle with paprika. Serve with lemon wedges.

Southern Fried Chicken and Gravy

Makes 8 servings

1 cup flour
½ teaspoon salt
½ teaspoon pepper
1 cup milk
2 eggs
2 3½-pound chickens, cut
  into serving pieces
  Peanut oil
3 tablespoons flour
1 pint half-and-half

Combine flour, salt, pepper, milk, and eggs; mix well. Dip chicken pieces in batter; set aside. Pour oil into a heavy skillet to a depth of 1 inch. Heat oil over medium heat to 350°. Gently place chicken skin-side down in skillet. Turn pieces as chicken begins to brown. When all pieces are lightly browned, reduce heat and cover. Cook for 25 to 30 minutes. Uncover and cook 10 to 15 minutes more or until large pieces are easily pierced with a fork. Drain chicken on paper towels; keep warm. Drain oil; reserve ¼ cup. Scrape pan to loosen browned flour bits. Heat reserved oil in skillet with browned bits. Whisk in 3 tablespoons flour; cook for 1 to 2 minutes or until flour is absorbed. Whisk in half-and-half; continue cooking over medium-high heat until thickened. Place chicken on serving platter; serve gravy separately.

Southern Fried Chicken, this page;
Cole Slaw, page 12

Sweet Potato Pie

Makes 6 servings

3 cups cooked sweet
  potatoes, puréed
¼ teaspoon each allspice,
  nutmeg, and salt
½ teaspoon cinnamon
1 cup firmly packed light
  brown sugar
3 eggs, lightly beaten
½ pint half-and-half
4 tablespoons butter, melted
1 9-inch pie crust, unbaked

Preheat oven to 450°. Place sweet potato purée in a large, deep mixing bowl. Blend in spices, sugar, and eggs. Mix in half-and-half and butter. Mound into prepared crust; press to edges. Bake 10 minutes; reduce heat to 250° and continue baking for 20 minutes or until pie tester inserted in center comes out clean. Sweet potato pie can be served hot or cold.

Corn Bread Dressing

Makes 8 servings

2½ cups day-old corn bread,
  crumbled
1½ cups coarse bread crumbs
1 large onion, minced
4 stalks celery, diced
1 red sweet pepper, seeded
  and chopped
4 tablespoons chopped
  fresh parsley
4 eggs, well beaten
4 cups chicken stock
1 teaspoon sage, optional
½ teaspoon salt
½ teaspoon crumbled dried
  thyme
¼ teaspoon pepper

Preheat oven to 350°. Grease a 1½-quart casserole. Combine all ingredients in a large bowl; mix well. Mound stuffing in prepared casserole. Bake uncovered for 1¼ hours or until golden brown. This dressing can be used to stuff chicken or turkey.

Scones

Makes 6 servings

1¾ cups flour
¼ teaspoon salt
2 teaspoons baking powder
5 tablespoons butter, cut
  into ½-inch pieces
½ cup sugar
1 egg, beaten
⅓ to ½ cup half-and-half

Preheat oven to 425°. Combine flour, salt, and baking powder in a deep mixing bowl. Using a pastry blender or a food processor fitted with a steel blade, cut butter into mixture until it resembles cornmeal. Mix in sugar, egg, and enough half-and-half to make a soft dough. Roll dough on a lightly floured board to ¾-inch thickness; cut 2 to 3-inch circles with a biscuit cutter or glass. Arrange scones on a greased cookie sheet. Bake for 10 to 12 minutes or until scones are golden brown. Serve warm with butter.

Hush Puppies
Makes 6 servings

2 cups cornmeal
1 small onion, minced
½ teaspoon salt
1 egg, beaten
1½ cups water
2 tablespoons butter, melted
½ cup vegetable oil *or* butter

Combine cornmeal, onion, and salt in a deep mixing bowl. Beat in egg and water; add butter. Set aside for 15 minutes. Heat oil in a large heavy skillet. Drop batter by tablespoonsful into skillet. Brown hush puppies on both sides. Serve hot.

Cracklin' Bread
Makes 6 to 8 servings

¾ cup diced slab bacon
2 cups cornmeal
2 teaspoons baking powder
1 cup buttermilk
2 eggs, well beaten

Preheat oven to 425°. Grease a 10-inch pie plate. Fry bacon in a large heavy skillet until crisp; drain. Reserve ¼ cup drippings. Combine cornmeal, baking powder, buttermilk, and eggs in a deep mixing bowl. Stir in drippings and bacon. Mound batter into prepared pie plate. Bake for 20 minutes or until a cake tester inserted in center comes out clean.

Candied Pecans
Makes 1 pound

1 cup sugar
¼ teaspoon salt
1 teaspoon vanilla
½ teaspoon cinnamon
1 pound shelled pecans
½ cup cold water

Combine all ingredients except pecans in a medium saucepan. Bring mixture to a boil; cook for 4 minutes, stirring often. Remove from heat; stir in pecans. Continue to stir until syrup forms a sugar coating over the pecans. Pour pecans on a cookie sheet; gently separate pecans while cooling.

Kentucky Derby Pie
Makes 6 to 8 servings

3 eggs, well beaten
¾ cup sugar
¼ teaspoon salt
1 cup butter, melted and cooled
1½ cups coarsely chopped pecans
1 tablespoon bourbon
2 tablespoons flour
1 cup semi-sweet chocolate chips
1 9 inch pie crust, unbaked

Preheat oven to 350°. Combine eggs, sugar, and salt in a large, deep mixing bowl. Blend in remaining ingredients, one at a time. Mound batter into pie crust. Cover pie with aluminum foil; bake for 20 minutes. Remove foil and continue baking for 25 to 30 minutes or until pie tester inserted in center comes out clean. Cool pie before serving.

Mississippi Mud Cake

Makes 8 servings

1 stick butter at room
temperature, cut into
1-inch pieces
1¾ cups sugar
4 eggs, slightly beaten
1¾ cups flour
⅓ cup cocoa
1 teaspoon vanilla
3½ cups miniature
marshmallows

Grease a 7 x 11-inch baking pan. Preheat oven to 350°. Cream butter and sugar in large mixing bowl until light and fluffy. Add eggs and continue beating until light. Add flour and cocoa; mix well. Add vanilla. Mound cake batter into prepared pan; smooth batter to edges with spatula. Bake for 30 minutes. Arrange marshmallows on top of cake, return to oven. Continue baking for 5 minutes or until marshmallows are melted. Set cake aside to cool. Prepare Frosting.

Frosting

1 stick butter at room
temperature, cut into ½-
inch pieces
1 1-pound box powdered
sugar, sifted
⅓ cup cocoa
½ cup heavy cream
½ teaspoon vanilla

Cream butter in a large bowl. Add sugar and cocoa; mix well. Blend in cream and vanilla until smooth. Frost cooled cake. Draw a knife through icing and melted marshmallow cream to create a marbling effect.

Cornpone

Makes 6 servings

2½ cups stone-ground
cornmeal
1½ cups flour
2 tablespoons dark
molasses
½ cup butter *or* shortening,
cut into ½-inch pieces
3 eggs, well beaten
2½ cups milk
Butter *or* warm honey

Preheat oven to 350°. Grease a corn stick pan; place pan in oven. Combine cornmeal, flour, and molasses in a deep mixing bowl. Cut in butter with a pastry blender or fork. Combine eggs and 1 cup milk in a separate bowl. Stir into the cornmeal mixture. Blend in remaining milk. Remove corn stick pan from oven and mound mixture into pan. Bake for 30 minutes or until golden brown. Serve with butter or warm honey.

Cornpone, this page

— Creole and Cajun —

Jambalaya

Makes 8 servings

4 tablespoons peanut oil
2 large onions, thinly sliced
5 stalks celery, sliced in
   ½-inch pieces
6 large tomatoes, chopped
3 tablespoons tomato paste
½ teaspoon paprika
3 bay leaves
1 tablespoon pickling spice
¼ teaspoon salt
⅛ teaspoon cayenne pepper
½ pound bulk sausage,
   sliced in ½-inch pieces
½ pound cooked ham, cut
   into ½-inch pieces
1 pound fresh scallops
8 fresh oysters, shucked
¾ pound fresh shrimp,
   shelled and deveined
3 cups long-grain rice
1 quart boiling water

Preheat oven to 375°. Heat oil in a large heavy skillet over medium heat; sauté onion and celery until tender, stirring occasionally. Mix in tomatoes, tomato paste, and seasonings. Bring mixture to a boil; add remaining ingredients, mixing well. Add boiling water; stir until blended. Cover pan securely and place in oven. Bake for 45 to 50 minutes or until rice is cooked, stirring occasionally. Discard bay leaves. Serve hot.

Blackened Redfish

Makes 6 servings

1 stick butter
4 tablespoons freshly
   squeezed lemon juice
   Salt and pepper
¼ teaspoon cayenne pepper
½ teaspoon crumbled dried
   thyme
2 pounds redfish or other
   fish fillets

Melt butter in a saucepan over medium heat. Stir in lemon juice and seasonings. Pour seasoned butter into a shallow dish. Heat a large, heavy iron skillet over high heat. Dip fillets into seasoned butter and fry quickly, turning once. The fillets will be charred on the outside. Transfer to a warmed platter. Add remaining seasoned butter to skillet, stirring to loosen browned bits on the bottom. Drizzle butter over fish. Open kitchen window during cooking if possible. This dish may also be made using prepared Blackened Redfish seasoning in place of the above seasonings.

Seafood Étouffée

Makes 6 servings

3 tablespoons butter
1 large clove garlic, minced
2 onions, thinly sliced
2 stalks celery, thinly sliced
¼ teaspoon crumbled dried
  rosemary
1 bay leaf
½ teaspoon Worcestershire
  sauce *or* to taste
¼ teaspoon Tabasco sauce
  Freshly squeezed juice of
  ½ lemon
2 pounds shrimp, *or*
  crawfish, shelled *or* fish
  fillets
¼ teaspoon salt
¼ teaspoon pepper
4 tablespoons minced fresh
  parsley
  Hot cooked rice

Heat butter in a large saucepan over medium heat. Sauté garlic, onion, and celery until tender, stirring occasionally. Stir in rosemary, bay leaf, Worcestershire sauce, Tabasco sauce, and lemon juice. Simmer covered for 10 minutes, stirring occasionally. Add seafood, salt, and pepper. Simmer for 10 to 15 minutes or until seafood is cooked. Do not overcook. Discard bay leaf. Sprinkle with parsley. Serve with hot rice.

Red Beans and Rice

Makes 8 servings

1 pound red beans, soaked
  in water overnight,
  drained, and water
  reserved
1 cup diced onion, divided
1 carrot, diced
½ teaspoon salt
2 bay leaves
1 ham bone
2 tablespoons oil
3 stalks celery, diced
1 teaspoon hot pepper
  sauce
½ teaspoon salt
¼ teaspoon cayenne pepper
1 cup long-grain rice
3 tablespoons peanut oil
1 teaspoon salt

Place beans in a large pan or Dutch oven with the reserved liquid and additional water to measure 6 cups liquid. Add ½ cup onion, carrot, salt, bay leaves, and ham bone. Cover and simmer beans 2½ hours, stirring occasionally. Heat oil in a heavy skillet; sauté celery and remaining onion until tender, stirring occasionally. Remove ham bone from beans; remove any ham and add to beans. Remove 1 cup beans; purée and return to pot. Add seasonings; keep warm. Place rice and 2 cups water, oil, and salt in a saucepan. Cook over medium heat until fluffy. Place a scoop of rice in a shallow bowl; ladle beans over rice. Serve hot.

Oyster Loaf
Makes 2 servings

1 dozen oysters, shucked
Salt and pepper
¾ cup cornmeal *or* corn
  flour, if available
1 cup vegetable oil *or* lard
1 9-inch loaf French bread
1 tablespoon butter at room
  temperature
4 tablespoons Tartar Sauce
  (See recipe on page 5)

Season oysters with salt and pepper to taste. Place cornmeal in a shallow dish; roll oysters in cornmeal. Pour vegetable oil into a large, deep, heavy skillet. Heat to 375°. Fry oysters in oil for about 1 minute on each side; drain on paper towels. Slice bread lengthwise to remove top quarter of the bread. Scoop out the white part leaving bottom and sides intact. Butter top and bottom of bread; toast under the broiler. Arrange fried oysters in toasted bread. Drizzle tartar sauce on top of oysters. Cover with top of loaf. Cut loaf in half. Serve immediately.

New Orleans French Toast
Makes 6 servings

6 eggs, well beaten
½ cup sugar
1 cup milk
12 slices French bread
4 to 5 tablespoons butter
  Powdered sugar
2 teaspoons grated lemon
  peel

Combine eggs, sugar, and milk in a shallow bowl. Soak the bread slices in this mixture for 20 minutes. Melt butter in a large heavy skillet over medium heat. Remove bread from egg mixture; fry on both sides until lightly brown. Sprinkle bread with powdered sugar and lemon peel.

Pecan Pie
Makes 6 to 8 servings

1 cup chopped pecans
1 9-inch pie crust, unbaked
2 eggs, beaten
1 cup dark corn syrup
½ cup firmly packed dark
  brown sugar
½ teaspoon cinnamon
½ cup raisins
1 teaspoon vanilla
½ cup pecan halves
3 tablespoons butter, cut
  into ½-inch pieces

Arrange chopped pecans in prepared pie crust. Preheat oven to 450°. Combine eggs, corn syrup, sugar, cinnamon, raisins, and vanilla in a deep bowl. Pour mixture over chopped pecans in crust. Arrange pecan halves over top of pie. Dot pie with butter. Bake for 10 minutes. Reduce heat to 325° and continue baking for 30 to 40 minutes until a pie tester inserted in center comes out clean. Cool pie before serving.

Pecan Pie, this page

Pecan Pralines

Makes 15 pralines

2 cups firmly packed dark
 brown sugar
½ cup milk
4 tablespoons butter
2 cups pecan halves

Combine sugar and milk in a heavy saucepan; cook over medium heat, stirring often, until mixture reaches soft-ball stage (234°). Remove pan from heat, let stand for 1 minute. Stir in butter and pecan halves; continue stirring until butter melts. Grease 2 feet of waxed paper; place on countertop. Drop praline batter by the tablespoonful onto waxed paper. Candy will harden as it cools. Store in airtight container.

Crème Brûlée

Makes 6 to 8 servings

8 egg yolks
¼ cup sugar
2 cups milk, scalded and
 cooled to room
 temperature
1 pint heavy cream, scalded
 and cooled to room
 temperature
1 teaspoon vanilla
½ cup firmly packed dark
 brown sugar, sifted

Preheat oven to 350°. Whisk together egg yolks and sugar in a large bowl until light. Add milk and cream in a slow steady stream. Stir in vanilla. Pour mixture into a deep 10-inch pie pan. Arrange pie pan in a larger baking dish filled with hot water to a depth of ½-inch. Bake in preheated oven for 2 hours or until a pie tester inserted in center comes out clean. Cool. Cover and refrigerate overnight. The day of serving preheat oven to broil. Sprinkle brown sugar over top of custard. Place custard in a larger baking dish filled with chopped ice and ice water to a depth of 1-inch. Place custard under broiler; broil for 2 to 3 minutes. Sugar will caramelize. Do not brown sugar. Remove pie plate from ice bath and wipe dry with paper towels; serve.

Black-Eyed Peas

Makes 8 to 10 servings

6 slices bacon, cut into
 ½-inch pieces
2 cloves garlic, minced
1 onion, minced
6 green onions, minced
¼ teaspoon Tabasco sauce
¼ teaspoon salt and pepper
 or to taste
1 pound dried black-eyed
 peas

Fry bacon in a large heavy skillet until crisp. Drain bacon on paper towels. Reheat drippings and sauté garlic, onion, and green onion until tender, stirring often. Transfer vegetables and drippings to a large saucepan. Add bacon and remaining ingredients; cover beans with boiling water. Bring mixture to a boil; reduce heat to simmer. Cover and cook for 2 hours, stirring occasionally. Add more water as needed until beans are cooked and all water is absorbed.

Shrimp Gumbo
Makes 6 to 8 servings

4 tablespoons butter
2 cloves garlic, minced
2 medium onions, minced
4 stalks celery, diced
1 green pepper, diced
3 tablespoons flour
1 28-ounce can tomatoes, chopped and juice reserved
1½ pounds shrimp in shells
1 pound fish fillets, cut into 2-inch pieces
¾ cup cooked ham, chopped
1 10-ounce package frozen okra, thawed
½ teaspoon salt
½ teaspoon crumbled dried thyme
¼ teaspoon pepper
¼ teaspoon chili powder
2 bay leaves
1 tablespoon filé powder
Hot rice

Heat butter in a large heavy skillet; sauté garlic, onion, celery, and pepper until tender, stirring occasionally. Whisk in flour and continue cooking until flour browns, stirring occasionally. Transfer vegetables to a large stockpot. Add all remaining ingredients except filé powder. Cover and simmer for 20 minutes. Discard bay leaves. Remove from heat and stir in filé powder. Serve gumbo in deep bowls over mounds of hot rice.

Dirty Rice
Makes 8 servings

4 slices bacon, cut into ½-inch pieces
2 onions, minced
1 red sweet pepper, seeded and chopped
3 stalks celery, diced
3 cloves garlic, minced
½ pound ground pork
½ pound chicken livers, puréed
2 bay leaves
¼ teaspoon crumbled dried thyme
¼ teaspoon each salt, pepper and red pepper flakes
4 cups hot cooked rice

Fry bacon in a large, heavy saucepan until crisp. Drain bacon on paper towels. Reheat drippings and sauté onion, pepper, celery, and garlic until tender, stirring occasionally. Add pork, liver purée, and spices. Sauté until meat is cooked (do not stir until meats are cooked). Simmer for 5 more minutes. Discard bay leaves. Toss meat mixture with hot rice in a deep bowl and serve hot.

Tex-Mex

Nachos
Makes 6 servings

½ cup vegetable oil
1 13⅓-ounce package large
  corn tortillas
  Garlic powder
½ pound sharp cheddar or
  Monterey jack, grated
  Chopped jalapeno
  peppers, optional

Heat oil in a small skillet to 375°. Hold tortillas firmly with tongs; fry for 5 seconds on each side. Drain on paper towels. Cut tortillas into quarters. Sprinkle with garlic powder to taste. Place on cookie sheet, sprinkle with cheese. Place nachos under broiler for 4 to 5 minutes or until the cheese melts. Garnish with jalapeno peppers; serve hot.

Barbecued Steak
Makes 6 servings

1 3-pound flank steak
2 cloves garlic, minced
¼ teaspoon salt
¼ teaspoon pepper
½ teaspoon crumbled dried
  oregano
¼ cup vegetable oil
¼ cup wine vinegar
2 teaspoons chopped
  cilantro

Cut steak into portions and rub the steak with minced garlic. Season with salt, pepper and oregano. Mix the oil and vinegar together in a shallow dish. Place steak in dish; marinate for 3 hours, turning occasionally. Grease rack of grill; place steaks on a hot grill about 4 inches from coals. Cook until desired degree of doneness is reached, turning once. Sprinkle with cilantro.

Chili with Tomatoes
Makes 8 servings

3 tablespoons bacon
  drippings
3 cloves garlic, peeled and
  minced
2 large onions, chopped
2 pounds chuck steak,
  coarsely ground
1 28-ounce can whole
  tomatoes, including juice
½ teaspoon salt
½ teaspoon pepper
2 tablespoons chili powder
1 tablespoon ground cumin
2 teaspoons honey
2 16-ounce cans kidney
  beans, including liquid
  Chopped onions
  Sour cream
  Tortillas

Heat bacon drippings in a large saucepan. Sauté garlic and onion until tender, stirring occasionally. Add ground chuck; fry until beef loses its color, stirring often. Quarter tomatoes; add tomatoes, juice, salt, pepper, chili powder, cumin, and honey to saucepan. Stir in beans. Simmer chili uncovered for 45 minutes, stirring occasionally. Adjust seasonings to taste. Serve with chopped onion, sour cream and fried tortillas.

Chili with Tomatoes, this page

Texas Smoked Brisket

Makes 8 servings

Soaked applewood *or*
mesquite wood chips
1 cup barbecue sauce
1 envelope dry onion soup
1 5½ to 6 pound beef
brisket, trimmed

Eight hours before serving time, start the fire in a smoker. Fill the fire pan with charcoal briquettes; start fire according to manufacturer's directions. When the coals are hot and gray-white in color, add drained wood pieces. Fill water pan with hot water; place in smoker. Mix 3 tablespoons barbecue sauce with onion mix and spread over top of the meat. Place brisket in center of smoker grill and cover. Smoke for 7 hours or until meat is cooked to desired degree of doneness. Check water pan and add water as needed every 2 hours. Slice brisket and serve with remaining barbecue sauce.

Huevos Rancheros

Makes 6 servings

3 tablespoons butter
1 large onion, minced
2 cloves garlic, minced
1 red sweet pepper, seeded
and chopped
1 pound ground chuck
1 tablespoon flour
½ cup beef stock
½ teaspoon salt
¼ teaspoon pepper
½ teaspoon crumbled dried
oregano, divided
6 eggs
1 large tomato, peeled,
seeded, and chopped
Warm tortillas

Melt 1 tablespoon butter in a large heavy skillet over medium heat. Sauté onion, garlic and pepper until tender, stirring occasionally. Add beef; cook until meat has browned and drain. Stir in flour, beef stock, salt, pepper, and ¼ teaspoon oregano; simmer for 5 minutes. Heat remaining butter in separate pan; fry eggs, sunny-side up. Arrange a portion of meat on each plate; place an egg on top of meat. Sprinkle each egg with tomatoes and oregano. Serve with warm tortillas.

Grilled Chicken Quarters

Makes 6 to 8 servings

½ pound fresh plums,
coarsely chopped *or* 1
17-ounce can, seeded
½ cup teriyaki sauce
2 cloves garlic, minced
1 tablespoon honey
2 3-pound chickens,
quartered

Purée plums in a blender or a food processor fitted with a steel blade; place in a deep bowl. Stir in teriyaki sauce, garlic, and honey. Place marinade in a large shallow dish. Place chicken quarters in dish; brush with sauce. Marinate for 4 hours, turning occasionally. Grease grill rack; arrange chicken on hot grill, about 5 inches from coals. Cook chicken 40 minutes or until done, turning pieces frequently; baste occasionally with marinade.

Enchiladas with Sour Cream

Makes 8 servings

3½ cups chopped, cooked chicken
2 medium onions, chopped
½ pint heavy cream
¾ cup vegetable oil
16 corn tortillas
2 cloves garlic, minced
6 large tomatoes, seeded and chopped
½ teaspoon crumbled dried oregano
¼ teaspoon salt
¼ teaspoon pepper
1 cup sour cream

Combine first 3 ingredients in a large mixing bowl; set aside. Heat oil in a medium skillet. Hold tortillas firmly with tongs, fry for 5 seconds on each side. Drain on paper towels. Purée remaining ingredients in a blender. Place in covered container and refrigerate until ready to use. Preheat oven to 350°. Dip tortillas in sauce. Place 3 tablespoons filling on each tortilla. Roll up each tortilla. Arrange, seam side down, in shallow 11 x 7-inch casserole. Drizzle remaining sauce over enchiladas. Bake uncovered for 20 minutes.

Chimichangas

Makes 6 servings

Chili Sauce (see recipe below)
2 cups chili, drained
6 10-inch flour tortillas
3 cups vegetable oil

Prepare Chili Sauce. Divide chili among the tortillas; spread evenly. Fold right and left sides of the tortilla over and ends under. Heat oil in a large skillet to 375°. Fry chimichangas, 2 at a time, folded side down. Fry 1 minute, or until golden brown on each side. Drain on paper towels. Serve warm with Chili Sauce.

Chili Sauce

Makes 1 cup

2 large tomatoes, peeled, seeded, and quartered
1 small onion, minced
2 canned mild peppers
4 sprigs cilantro
½ cup chicken stock
½ teaspoon Tabasco

Combine all ingredients in a blender or a food processor fitted with a steel blade. Place in a covered container and chill until ready to serve.

Refried Beans

Makes 6 servings

4 tablespoons bacon drippings
1 large onion, minced
2 cloves garlic, minced
3 cups cooked black beans or pinto beans, puréed
½ teaspoon ground cumin
½ teaspoon salt
¼ teaspoon pepper

Heat bacon drippings in a heavy skillet. Sauté onion and garlic over medium heat until tender. Stir in beans. Season with cumin, salt, and pepper. Cook about 10 minutes or until thick and heated.

Tostados
Makes 6 servings

1 cup vegetable oil
6 corn tortillas
2 cups refried beans
2 cups shredded lettuce
½ pound ground beef, cooked
  Bottled taco sauce
1 onion, minced
1 large tomato, chopped
  Sliced black olives, chili peppers, and shredded cheese

Heat oil in a small skillet to 375°. Hold tortillas firmly with tongs; fry for 5 seconds on each side. Drain on paper towels. Arrange a tortilla on each plate. Spread refried beans over tortillas; sprinkle with ground beef and shredded lettuce. Top with a dollop of taco sauce; sprinkle with minced onion, tomato, olives, peppers, and cheese. Serve immediately.

Guacamole
Makes 6 servings

3 large ripe avocados, peeled, pits reserved
1 small onion, chopped
2 cloves garlic, minced
1 tomato, peeled, seeded, and chopped
3 sprigs cilantro
½ teaspoon Tabasco sauce
2 teaspoons lime juice
  Nachos or vegetables cut into bite-size pieces

Purée avocado in food processor fitted with steel blade or use a blender. Add remaining ingredients; purée. Arrange guacamole in a serving bowl and serve with nachos or cut vegetables. If guacamole will be served later, place avocado pits in bowl; remove before serving. The pits help to prevent discoloration. Cover and refrigerate until ready to serve.

Flan
Makes 6 servings

6 tablespoons sugar
6 eggs, well beaten
1 teaspoon vanilla
1 teaspoon finely grated lemon peel
¼ teaspoon salt
¼ cup sugar
3 cups scalded milk

Preheat oven to 350°. Place sugar and 3 tablespoons water in a 1-quart mold. Place mold over medium heat until sugar begins to brown. Remove from heat; tip mold to coat bottom and sides. Set aside to cool. Combine eggs, vanilla, lemon peel, salt, and sugar in a large bowl. Stir in milk; strain mixture through a sieve into prepared mold. Carefully place mold into a large pan. Pour hot water into pan to a depth of 1 inch. Bake for 1½ hours or until cake tester inserted in center comes out clean. Remove mold from water-filled pan; cool to room temperature. Refrigerate until ready to serve; unmold flan onto platter.

Tostados, this page

The Midwest

Potato Soup

Makes 6 servings

5 tablespoons butter
2 onions, minced
3 cups potatoes, diced
5 cups chicken stock
½ teaspoon white pepper
½ teaspoon salt
2 cups chopped watercress
½ pint heavy cream
Chopped chives

Heat butter in a large saucepan over medium heat. Sauté onion until tender, stirring occasionally. Add potatoes, chicken stock, and seasonings. Bring soup to a boil; reduce heat. Simmer for 10 minutes or until potatoes are soft. Stir in watercress; simmer for 4 minutes. Purée soup in blender. Return to saucepan; stir in heavy cream and reheat. Serve sprinkled with chopped chives.

Corn-Tomato Soup

Makes 6 servings

4 tablespoons butter
2 onions, minced
1 clove garlic, minced
3 cups corn, cut from
  the ear
4 cups chicken stock
2 tomatoes, chopped
¼ teaspoon each oregano,
  salt, and white pepper

Heat butter in large saucepan over medium heat. Sauté onion and garlic until tender, stirring occasionally. Sauté corn for 3 minutes, stirring occasionally. Mix in chicken stock, tomatoes, and seasonings. Bring mixture to a boil; reduce heat to simmer. Cook for 15 minutes or until soup is hot.

Cornish Pasties

Makes 6 servings

1 pound chuck steak,
  coarsely ground
2 cups diced potatoes
1 carrot, grated
2 onions, peeled
1 stalk celery, chopped
1 teaspoon Worcestershire
  sauce
½ teaspoon salt
¼ teaspoon pepper
3 cups flour
½ teaspoon salt
¾ cup shortening or lard at
  room temperature
  Ice water
1 egg, slightly beaten

Preheat oven to 350°. Combine first 8 ingredients in a large mixing bowl; reserve. Combine flour and salt in a separate bowl. Cut in shortening with a pastry blender. Sprinkle the dough with 5 to 7 tablespoons ice water. Blend the water in until dough holds together. Form dough into a ball. Divide into 6 equal portions. On a lightly floured board roll each dough ball into a 6 to 7-inch circle. Divide filling into 6 portions; place on each dough circle. Fold dough in half over meat mixture and press the edges together to seal. Prick dough with tines of a fork. Arrange pasties on an ungreased cookie sheet. Brush tops of pasties with beaten egg. Bake for 40 minutes or until a golden brown. Serve warm.

Beef Wellington
Makes 6 to 8 servings

Crust

2¼ cups flour
1 teaspoon salt, divided
¼ cup butter, cut into ½-inch pieces
¼ cup shortening
Ice water

Combine flour and ½ teaspoon salt in a large bowl. Cut in butter and shortening with pastry blender or food processor fitted with steel blade until mixture resembles coarse crumbs. Sprinkle the dough with 3 tablespoons of ice water. Blend the water in, tossing lightly with a fork until the dough clings together. Form dough into a ball. Knead for 1 minute on a lightly floured board. Cover with plastic wrap and refrigerate at least 1 hour. Prepare Vegetable Filling.

Vegetable Filling

½ pound mushrooms, minced
3 tablespoons butter
1 onion, minced
3 stalks celery, minced
¼ cup chopped fresh parsley
2 tablespoons flour
½ teaspoon salt
Pepper
¼ cup red wine

Squeeze excess moisture from mushrooms with paper towels. Melt butter in a large skillet. Sauté onion and celery until tender, stirring occasionally. Add mushrooms and parsley; cook until tender. Stir in flour, salt, pepper to taste, and wine, blending well. Simmer for 2 minutes, stir and set aside. Prepare Beef Tenderloin.

Beef Tenderloin

5 tablespoons butter
4 pounds lean beef tenderloin
¼ cup Madeira

Preheat oven to 425°. Melt butter in a shallow roasting pan. Place meat in pan; roast for 25 minutes, basting with Madeira. Remove from oven and set meat aside.

To Assemble: Preheat oven to 400°. Generously grease a baking sheet. Remove dough from refrigerator and divide into two portions. Roll out each portion on a lightly floured surface. Roll into a ¼-inch thick rectangle 1½ inches longer and wider than fillet. Place one rectangle on prepared baking sheet. Place tenderloin in center of rectangle. Spread vegetable filling evenly over top of tenderloin. Carefully place remaining dough rectangle over top. Bring upper and lower edges together; press edges together to seal. Remove excess dough. Re-roll remaining dough. Cut out decorative designs; using a small amount of water, press designs on top of crust. Bake for 40 to 45 minutes or until pastry is golden brown. Let stand for 15 minutes before slicing.

Chicken Pie

Makes 6 servings

¾ cup flour
1 teaspoon crumbled dried dill
¼ teaspoon salt
¼ cup shortening
Chicken Filling (see recipe below)

Combine dry ingredients in a deep bowl; cut in shortening with pastry blender until dough resembles coarse cornmeal. Sprinkle 1 to 3 tablespoons of ice water over dry ingredients; mix gently until dough forms a ball. Cover with plastic wrap and chill for 1 hour before rolling out. Prepare Chicken Filling.

Chicken Filling

1 cup diced celery
½ cup diced onion
5 tablespoons butter
5 tablespoons flour
½ cup chicken stock
1 cup half-and-half
½ teaspoon salt
¼ teaspoon white pepper
¼ teaspoon crumbled dried rosemary
3 tablespoons chopped fresh parsley, divided
1 cup diced tomatoes
2½ cups cooked diced chicken
½ pound mushrooms, thinly sliced
1 10-ounce package frozen peas, thawed and drained
2 cups mashed potatoes
Paprika

Combine celery and onion in a saucepan with boiling salted water. Cook vegetables over medium heat about 15 minutes or until tender-crisp; drain well. Melt butter in a separate saucepan; whisk in flour. Cook 2 to 3 minutes or until flour is absorbed. Whisk in stock, half-and-half, salt, pepper, rosemary, and 2 tablespoons parsley. Continue to whisk until mixture thickens; cool. Stir in drained vegetables, tomatoes, chicken, mushrooms, and peas. Preheat oven to 375°. Roll pastry out to fit a deep 9-inch pie pan. Spoon filling into crust. Pipe mashed potatoes around edges and in the center. Sprinkle with remaining parsley and paprika. Bake for 30 to 45 minutes or until crust is done and tops of potatoes are lightly browned.

Veal Cutlets

Makes 6 servings

½ cup flour
½ teaspoon salt
½ teaspoon crumbled dried basil
¼ teaspoon pepper
¼ teaspoon garlic powder
2 eggs, slightly beaten
1½ pounds veal cutlets
1 cup bread crumbs
1 stick butter, divided
6 eggs

Place flour in a shallow bowl; mix in salt, basil, pepper, and garlic powder. Place beaten eggs in a shallow bowl. Dredge veal pieces in flour mixture and dip in eggs. Place on a sheet of waxed paper; dust both sides with bread crumbs. Set aside for 5 minutes. Heat ⅔ stick of butter in a large heavy skillet. Fry veal cutlets on both sides until tender and golden brown. Remove from skillet and keep warm. Heat butter in skillet; fry eggs. Arrange veal cutlets on each plate and top with a fried egg.

Chicken Pie, this page

Potato Salad
Makes 6 to 8 servings

2¼ pounds red potatoes
½ cup mayonnaise
½ cup sour cream
3 tablespoons chopped
  fresh parsley
1 teaspoon white
  horseradish
¼ teaspoon white pepper
5 hard-boiled eggs, chopped
1 large onion, minced

Cook potatoes in salted water until tender; drain and slice. Arrange potatoes in a deep serving bowl. Combine remaining ingredients in a small bowl; toss potatoes with dressing. Cover and refrigerate for 2 hours before serving.

Iowa Corn Fritters
Makes 6 servings

2 cups freshly grated corn
2 eggs, slightly beaten
2 tablespoons flour
1 teaspoon baking powder
½ teaspoon salt
¼ teaspoon pepper
1 small onion, minced
5 tablespoons butter
  Honey

Combine all ingredients in a medium mixing bowl except butter and honey. Let batter stand at room temperature for 10 minutes. Heat butter in a heavy skillet. Drop batter from a tablespoon; fry until lightly brown on both sides. Serve with honey.

Wild Rice
Makes 6 servings

3 tablespoons butter
1 onion, chopped
5 stalks celery, thinly sliced
½ pound mushrooms, thinly
  sliced
1½ cups wild rice
½ teaspoon salt
¼ teaspoon pepper
4½ cups chicken stock

Preheat oven to 375°. Melt butter in a deep heavy skillet. Sauté onion, celery and mushrooms until tender, stirring occasionally. Add rice; toss with vegetables. Add salt, pepper, and stock. Pour rice mixture into a greased 1½-quart casserole. Cover tightly and bake for 1½ hours. Add more liquid if needed during baking.

Raisin Crumb Pie

Makes 6 servings

2 cups dark raisins, chopped
2½ cups sugar, divided
1½ cups flour
1 tablespoon freshly grated
  lemon peel
6 tablespoons butter, cut
  into ½-inch pieces
2 eggs, beaten
1 cup milk
1 teaspoon vanilla
1 9-inch pie crust, unbaked

Combine raisins and 2 cups boiling water in a medium saucepan; bring to a boil over medium heat. Reduce heat to simmer and cook for 10 minutes. Drain; stir in 1½ cups sugar. Mix together flour, remaining sugar, and grated peel in a mixing bowl. Cut in butter with a pastry blender; set aside 1¼ cups for topping. Add eggs, milk, and vanilla to the remaining mixture. Preheat oven to 450°. Spoon raisins into pie crust. Pour egg mixture over raisins; sprinkle reserved crumbs over top of pie. Bake for 10 minutes. Reduce heat to 350°; continue baking for 20 to 25 minutes or until a pie tester inserted in center comes out clean.

Lemon Meringue Bread Pudding

Makes 6 servings

3 cups crumbled day-old
  bread
3 cups milk
4 eggs, separated, yolks
  slightly beaten
1 cup sugar, divided
¼ teaspoon each salt,
  nutmeg, freshly grated
  lemon peel
1½ teaspoons lemon extract

Preheat oven to 325°. Place bread pieces in a deep mixing bowl. Cover with milk; let stand until bread is soft. Stir in egg yolks, ⅔ cup sugar, salt, nutmeg, and grated lemon peel; blend well. Pour mixture into a greased 1½-quart baking dish; place dish in a shallow pan filled with hot water to a depth of 1 inch. Bake for 1¼ hours or until pudding is lightly browned and pulling away from sides of pan. Beat egg whites until stiff but not dry; gradually beat in remaining sugar. Add lemon extract. Spread meringue over bread pudding. Bake 15 minutes more or until meringue is slightly browned.

Spiced Crab Apples

Makes 6 to 8 servings

2 cups sugar
2 cups wine vinegar
3 medium cinnamon sticks
1 teaspoon whole cloves
2 pounds crab apples,
  washed and drained
  (discard any apples with
  blemishes)

Combine all ingredients except apples in a large pot; bring to a boil over medium heat. Continue to cook for 5 minutes, stirring often. Add the apples; return to a boil. Reduce heat; simmer for 10 minutes or until apples are tender. Remove from heat. Cover pot; cool. Remove apples to a deep bowl. Reheat liquid; boil until it forms a thick syrup. Drizzle syrup over apples; cool.

Lamb Kabobs

Makes 6 servings

¼ cup soy sauce
¼ cup honey
2 tablespoons salad oil
1 tablespoon lemon *or* lime juice
2 cloves garlic, minced
2½ pounds lamb, cut into 1½-inch cubes
3 green or red sweet peppers, cut into wedges
½ pound pearl onions
½ pound large mushrooms, stems removed
1 pound cherry tomatoes
6 skewers

Combine first 5 ingredients in a shallow bowl; marinate lamb pieces for 2 hours, turning occasionally. Thread skewers alternating lamb, pepper, onions, mushrooms and tomatoes. Cook over hot charcoals for 15 minutes; turn and baste occasionally. Cook 10 to 15 minutes longer.

Barbecued Lamb Riblets

Makes 6 servings

5 pounds lamb riblets, trimmed of extra fat
¾ cup firmly packed dark brown sugar
1 teaspoon dry mustard
3 tablespoons wine vinegar
½ teaspoon salt
½ teaspoon Tabasco sauce
½ cup catsup
2 cloves garlic, minced

Place ribs in a large pot; cover with water. Cook until soft; drain. Set aside to cool. Combine remaining ingredients; brush ribs with ½ the sauce. Place ribs in a baking dish; pour remaining sauce over. Place ribs in refrigerator overnight. When ready to serve, bake ribs uncovered at 325° for 45 minutes or until crisp, turning occasionally.

Smoked Turkey

Makes 8 servings

Soaked mesquite *or* cherry wood chips
1 12 to 13-pound turkey, thawed
Salt, pepper, and garlic powder

Fill the fire pan of a smoker grill with charcoal briquettes; start fire according to the manufacturer's directions. When coals are hot and gray-white in color, add drained wood pieces. Fill water pan with hot water; place in smoker. Sprinkle turkey with salt, pepper, and garlic powder; place turkey in center of grill and cover. Smoke for 11 to 12 hours or until turkey is cooked. Check water pan and add water as needed every 2 hours.

Turkey Hash

Makes 6 servings

4 cups diced cooked turkey
1½ cups diced cooked
    potatoes
1 large onion, minced
5 tablespoons butter
¼ teaspoon each salt,
    paprika, and garlic powder
4 tablespoons chopped
    fresh parsley

Toss turkey, potatoes, and onion in a large, deep mixing bowl. Heat butter in a large heavy skillet over medium heat. Brown turkey mixture; season with salt, paprika, and garlic powder. Cook until edges brown. Add more butter if needed. Place in a deep bowl and sprinkle with chopped parsley.

Red-Flannel Hash

Makes 6 servings

6 strips bacon, cut into
    ½-inch pieces
1 onion, minced
3 cups cooked, ground
    corned beef
1 cup diced cooked beets
3½ cups diced cooked
    potatoes
4 to 6 tablespoons heavy
    cream
½ teaspoon pepper
¼ teaspoon garlic powder

Fry bacon in large heavy skillet until crisp; drain on paper towels. Discard all but 3 tablespoons of bacon drippings. Reheat drippings; sauté onion until tender, stirring occasionally. Remove onion and toss with remaining ingredients in a deep mixing bowl. Reheat drippings again and place hash into skillet. Cook over medium heat; turn with spatula to prevent sticking. Cook for 20 minutes or until hash is cooked and slightly browned.

Roasted Corn in the Husk

Makes 6 servings

12 ears fresh corn
    Butter
    Salt

Loosen husks and remove silk from each ear of corn. Fill a bucket with water, dip each ear of corn in the water, and shake dry. Tighten husks around corn; arrange corn on grill over hot coals. Roast corn for about 10 to 15 minutes, turning as often as needed, until corn is cooked. Remove husks and serve hot. Serve with butter and salt.

Skillet Chicken with Fruit

Makes 6 servings

3½-pounds chicken pieces
1 cup flour
4 tablespoons butter
2 tablespoons vegetable oil
1½ cups orange juice
½ cup pineapple juice
½ teaspoon salt
¼ teaspoon cloves
¼ teaspoon nutmeg
3 tablespoons butter
2 tablespoons flour
1 cup pineapple chunks, drained
1 cup orange slices
Cooked rice

Dredge chicken pieces in flour. Heat butter and oil in a large heavy skillet over medium heat. Brown chicken on all sides. Lower heat and cook for 30 minutes. Combine ½ cup orange juice and ¼ cup pineapple juice with seasonings. Pour juice over chicken. Cover and simmer until chicken is tender. Heat butter in a small saucepan; whisk in flour and cook for 2 to 3 minutes or until flour is absorbed. Add remaining orange juice and pineapple juice; simmer until sauce thickens. Stir in fruit and pour sauce over chicken. Simmer uncovered for 5 minutes. Serve hot over rice.

Wilted Salad

Makes 6 servings

5 slices bacon
3 tablespoons freshly squeezed lemon juice
1 teaspoon sugar
¼ teaspoon salt
2 red onions, thinly sliced
1 medium head lettuce
4 oranges, peeled and sectioned
¾ cup diced Swiss cheese

Fry bacon in heavy skillet until crisp; drain and crumble. Leave drippings in pan; reheat. Add lemon juice, sugar, salt, and onion; sauté over medium heat until onions are tender. Tear lettuce into bite-sized pieces and place in salad bowl. Pour the hot mixture over lettuce. Toss with fried bacon, orange sections, and Swiss cheese. Serve immediately.

French-Fried Onion Rings

Makes 6 servings

6 large onions, sliced in rings ¼ inch thick
2 cups milk
Flour
Salt and pepper
Vegetable oil

Separate rings and arrange in shallow bowl. Cover with milk and let stand for 20 minutes. Drain onions; toss with flour, salt, and pepper. Heat oil in an electric fryer or a large heavy skillet to 375°. Cook onion rings in batches until golden brown. Drain on paper towels. Continue until all onion rings are cooked.

Banana Bread

Makes 1 loaf

1 cup sugar
1 stick butter, cut into ½-inch
　pieces
2 eggs, well beaten
3 ripe bananas, puréed
3 tablespoons sour cream
2¾ cups flour
1 teaspoon baking soda
1 teaspoon baking powder
1 teaspoon vanilla
¾ cup chopped walnuts

Preheat oven to 350°. Grease a 9 x 5-inch loaf pan. Beat sugar and butter in a large bowl until light and fluffy. Add eggs; continue beating until light. Blend in remaining ingredients one at a time until batter is smooth. Mound into prepared pan; bake for 50 to 55 minutes or until cake tester inserted in center comes out clean. Cool on wire rack. Slice and serve.

Prune Cake

Makes 6 servings

1 cup sugar
¾ cup butter *or* shortening
3 eggs, slightly beaten
½ cup sour cream
1½ cups chopped cooked
　prunes
2 cups flour
¼ teaspoon nutmeg
¼ teaspoon cloves
½ teaspoon cinnamon
1 teaspoon baking soda
¼ teaspoon baking powder

Preheat oven to 350°. Grease a 9-inch square baking pan or a 9 x 5-inch loaf pan. Cream sugar and butter in a large bowl until light and fluffy. Add eggs; continue beating until light. Blend in sour cream and prunes; mix in dry ingredients. Mound batter into prepared pan. Bake for 40 minutes or until cake tester inserted in center comes out clean. Cool on wire rack. Serve warm or cold.

Fruit Cobbler

Makes 6 to 8 servings

3 cups thinly sliced peaches
2 cups blueberries
1 tablespoon lime juice
¼ teaspoon nutmeg
¼ teaspoon cinnamon
2 cups flour
4 tablespoons sugar
2 teaspoons baking powder
¼ teaspoon salt
2 tablespoons butter, melted
1 cup milk
　Whipped cream

Preheat oven to 375°. Arrange peach slices and blueberries in a greased, deep, 10-inch pie plate. Sprinkle with lime juice, nutmeg, and cinnamon. Mix dry ingredients in a separate bowl. Blend in butter and milk; spoon mixture by the tablespoonful over fruit. Bake cobbler for 30 minutes or until the top is golden brown. Cool slightly. Serve with whipped cream.

Backyard Clambake, page 6; Sourdough Bread, page 57; Cole Slaw, page 12

California

Spinach Salad

Makes 6 servings

1 pound spinach, washed
   and stems removed
6 slices bacon
¼ cup wine vinegar
2 tablespoons light brown
   sugar
¼ teaspoon salt
   Freshly ground pepper to
   taste
¾ pound cooked shrimp
4 hard-boiled eggs, chopped
½ pound mushrooms, sliced

Tear spinach into bite-sized pieces; place in a deep salad bowl. Fry bacon in a heavy skillet over medium heat until crisp. Crumble bacon; reserve. Drain all but 3 tablespoons hot bacon drippings. Add vinegar, sugar, salt, and pepper to drippings. Reheat dressing; set aside. Toss salad with remaining ingredients, mix in hot dressing. Serve immediately.

Seviche

Makes 6 servings

1½ pounds scallops, cut into
   ½-inch cubes
   Freshly squeezed lemon
   and lime juice
1 large tomato, diced
1 red onion, thinly sliced
   and separated into rings
1 4-ounce can green chilies,
   drained
3 tablespoons chopped
   cilantro
   Salt and pepper to taste
   Lettuce leaves

Place scallops in a glass bowl. Cover scallops with a combination of lemon and lime juice; toss. Add remaining ingredients except lettuce; toss. Cover seviche and refrigerate overnight, turning scallops at least twice. Place lettuce leaves on individual plates; mound seviche in center. Serve chilled.

Taco Salad

Makes 6 servings

1 medium head lettuce, torn
   into small pieces
2 cups chili
¾ cup sliced black olives
¾ cup grated Monterey jack
   cheese
2 large tomatoes, cut in
   wedges
1 onion, thinly sliced
1 15-ounce can garbanzos,
   drained
2 avocados, pitted and
   sliced
   Tortilla chips

Arrange lettuce in a large, deep salad bowl. Toss chili with olives and place in center of bowl. Arrange remaining ingredients around edges of bowl. Toss salad at table.

Artichokes
Makes 6 servings

2 tablespoons vegetable oil
2 tablespoons lemon juice, divided
1 clove garlic, minced
½ teaspoon salt
6 large firm artichokes, trimmed, tips of each leaf cut off and dipped in lemon juice
1 stick butter at room temperature
2 tablespoons chopped fresh parsley
¼ teaspoon Worcestershire sauce

Fill a large pot two-thirds full with water; add all ingredients except artichokes. Bring water to a boil over medium-high heat; add artichokes. Reduce heat to simmer; cover and continue cooking for 30 minutes, or until a leaf can be pulled off easily and base of artichoke can be pierced with a fork. Do not overcook. Drain upside down on paper towels before serving. Remove the center (choke). Melt butter in a small saucepan over medium-low heat. Mix in remaining ingredients until blended. Serve sauce warm.

Fresh Fruit Platter
Makes 6 to 8 servings

3 cups cubed and seeded watermelon
1 pint strawberries
1 papaya, peeled, seeded, and sliced
2 kiwis, peeled and sliced
1 pineapple, cut into chunks
1 large orange
Strawberry Sauce (see recipe below)

Arrange fruit decoratively on platter. Any variety of fresh fruits can be substituted, according to availability. Cut top off orange; discard. Cut edges zigzag style with small fruit knife. Hollow out orange. Place orange in center of fruit platter. Prepare Strawberry Sauce; fill orange with sauce. Cover; chill platter until ready to serve.

Strawberry Sauce

1 cup strawberries, puréed
1 cup plain yogurt
2 teaspoons honey
1 teaspoon chopped candied ginger

Combine all ingredients in a small bowl. Adjust seasonings to taste.

Seafood-Stuffed Artichokes

Makes 6 servings

4 tablespoons butter
3 stalks celery, chopped
1 onion, minced
4 tablespoons chopped
  fresh parsley
2 tablespoons flour
¼ teaspoon each salt, white
  pepper, and garlic powder
½ pint heavy cream
2 cups diced cooked
  seafood
6 large artichokes, cooked

Heat butter in a large heavy skillet over medium heat; sauté celery and onion until tender, stirring occasionally. Add in parsley and flour; whisk until flour is absorbed. Add seasonings and cream; continue cooking until sauce thickens slightly. Add seafood; cook until seafood is heated through. Spoon mixture into warm artichokes; serve immediately.

Oyster Soup

Makes 4 to 6 servings

5 tablespoons butter
3 green onions, chopped
2 stalks celery, minced
2 tablespoons flour
2 dozen oysters, chopped
  with liquid reserved
2 cups half-and-half
1 teaspoon chopped fresh
  parsley
¼ teaspoon salt
¼ teaspoon white pepper

Heat butter in a medium saucepan; sauté vegetables over medium heat, stirring occasionally. Stir in flour and oysters; continue cooking, whisking constantly, until flour is absorbed. Stir in half-and-half and reserved oyster juice; simmer for 10 minutes. Season with parsley, salt, and pepper. Serve in small bowls.

Gazpacho

Makes 6 servings

5 large tomatoes, peeled
  and quartered
2 cucumbers, peeled and
  sliced
¼ green pepper, chopped
1 small onion, quartered
2 cloves garlic
1 cup tomato juice or
  bouillon
4 tablespoons olive oil
3 tablespoons wine vinegar
2 slices white bread, crusts
  removed and cubed
¼ teaspoon pepper
  Green pepper rings

Purée all ingredients except green pepper rings in blender or food processor fitted with steel blade. Purée in batches until smooth; combine in a deep bowl. Cover; chill. Soup will be thick but not solid. Serve Gazpacho in bowls topped with green pepper rings.

Gazpacho, this page

Veal with Ginger

Makes 4 servings

1 2-inch piece of fresh
   ginger, cut in fine strips
¼ cup water
1 tablespoon sugar
1½ pounds veal cutlets, cut
   into 4 portions
4 tablespoons flour
4 tablespoons butter
2 large tomatoes, peeled
   and chopped
¾ pint heavy cream
1 tablespoon grated lemon
   peel
   Lemon slices
   Parsley sprigs

Place ginger in a small saucepan with water and sugar. Boil until all of the water has evaporated; set aside. Pound veal flat between two pieces of waxed paper; dust veal with flour. Heat butter in a large heavy skillet until hot; sauté veal cutlets for approximately 1 minute on each side. Do not overcook. Place veal on a heated platter; cover with aluminum foil. Reheat drippings in skillet; stir in chopped tomatoes. Cook over medium heat, scraping all particles of food from skillet; cook until tomatoes are dry. Add cream; simmer until mixture thickens slightly. Stir in candied ginger. Place veal on individual plates; ladle sauce over veal. Sprinkle with grated lemon peel. Serve with lemon slices and parsley sprigs.

Goat Cheese Pizza

Makes 4 small pizzas

1 package active dry yeast
½ teaspoon honey
½ teaspoon salt
1½ teaspoons olive oil
4 cups flour
2 cups whole-wheat flour
4 tablespoons cornmeal
1 pound goat cheese,
   crumbled
1 pound sweet Italian
   sausage, thinly sliced,
   casing discarded
4 small red sweet peppers,
   seeded and sliced
½ teaspoon crumbled dried
   sage

Place 2 cups warm water (105° to 115°) in a large bowl. Sprinkle yeast over water; blend together. Set aside in a draft-free area for 5 minutes until bubbly. Stir in honey, salt, and olive oil. Add flour slowly to mixture, mixing by hand or using electric mixer with dough hook attachment until all flour is used. Knead dough until smooth, about 4 to 5 minutes. Place dough in a greased bowl; turn once. Place in a draft-free area for 1 hour or until doubled in size. Punch dough down and divide into 4 equal balls. Set aside for 30 minutes or until double in bulk. Thinly roll each ball of dough out into a circle. Place crust on pizza pans or cookie sheets dusted with cornmeal. Arrange clay tiles on oven rack in the center of oven. Preheat oven to 500°. Sprinkle cheese, sausage, and peppers evenly over crust. Sprinkle with sage. Arrange pans on tiles. Bake for approximately 5 to 10 minutes, or until crust is crisp and golden and cheese is melted. Slice and serve hot.

Sourdough Bread

Makes 2 loaves

1 package active dry yeast
1 cup boiling water
2 tablespoons sugar
2 tablespoons butter at
  room temperature
1½ cups Sourdough Starter
  (see recipe below)
½ teaspoon salt
1 teaspoon white vinegar
4½ cups flour
1 tablespoon cornmeal
1 egg white

Combine yeast with ¼ cup warm water (105° to 115°) in a small glass bowl. Stir; set aside for 5 minutes in a draft-free area. Combine boiling water with sugar and butter in a separate bowl. Cool mixture until warm; add yeast mixture, Sourdough Starter, and salt. Add vinegar and 2 cups flour; mix together for 2 minutes or until the ingredients begin to form a dough. Work remaining flour into dough by kneading on a lightly floured board for 5 to 8 minutes or until dough is smooth. Place dough in a large greased bowl; turn dough once. Cover loosely; let rise for 1½ hours in a draft-free area or until doubled in bulk. Punch dough down; divide dough in half and place on lightly floured board. Form into two log shapes. Place loaves in greased bread pans sprinkled with cornmeal. Cover bread lightly; set aside for 1¼ hours or until double in bulk. Preheat oven to 400°. Cut slashes diagonally in loaves. Combine egg white with 2 tablespoons warm water; brush tops of bread with mixture. Bake for 35 minutes or until browned and cake tester inserted in center comes out clean. Cool on rack.

Sourdough Starter

Makes 2 cups starter

1 package active dry yeast
2 cups flour

Combine yeast, flour, and 2 cups warm water (105° to 115°) in a glass bowl. Cover bowl; set aside at room temperature for 48 hours. Stir mixture twice each day. The starter will be bubbling. Refrigerate mixture after 48 hours. Stir mixture well before using. Ladle out amount required in recipe. Replenish the remaining starter each time by mixing in 1 cup flour and 1 cup warm water. Let starter stand uncovered in a warm area for 4 hours or until it begins to bubble. Cover loosely and refrigerate. Use and replenish within two weeks for continuing yeast action.

Poached Salmon with Hollandaise Sauce

Makes 6 servings

¼ cup firmly packed dark
    brown sugar
1 onion, minced
3 cloves garlic, minced
¼ teaspoon freshly ground
    black pepper
½ teaspoon crumbled dried
    oregano
2 cups dry white wine
2¼ pounds salmon steaks cut
    into serving pieces
    Hollandaise Sauce (see
    recipe below)

Combine all ingredients except salmon in a shallow dish. Place salmon steaks in dish; marinate for 6 hours in refrigerator, turning occasionally. Remove from marinade; pat dry with paper towels. Place marinade and 1 quart water in a large pan or poacher; bring to a boil. Tie salmon in cheesecloth; place in boiling marinade. Simmer for about 12 minutes or until bone can be lifted out cleanly. Remove salmon; place on serving platter. Serve hot with Hollandaise Sauce.

Hollandaise Sauce

½ cup butter, creamed and at
    room temperature
4 egg yolks
1 tablespoon freshly
    squeezed lemon juice
    Salt
2 tablespoons boiling water

Place creamed butter in top of double boiler over warm water. Beat in egg yolks one at a time; add lemon juice and salt to taste. Whisk in boiling water; stir until thickened.

Pork Chops with Apple Rings

Makes 6 servings

¼ teaspoon salt
¼ teaspoon pepper
½ cup flour
½ cup seasoned bread
    crumbs
6 1-inch thick pork chops,
    trimmed
4 tablespoons shortening
4 tablespoons butter
2 tablespoons freshly
    squeezed lemon juice
6 apples, sliced in rings

Mix salt, pepper, flour, and bread crumbs in a paper bag. Place pork chops in bag; shake to coat. Heat 2 tablespoons of shortening in a large heavy skillet; brown chops until cooked, about 6 minutes on each side. Remove chops from skillet; keep warm. Reheat remaining drippings; add butter over medium heat. Sprinkle lemon juice over apple slices. Fry apple slices until tender-crisp and golden brown on both sides. Do not overcook. Serve pork chops with apple slices.

Poached Salmon with Hollandaise,
this page

Salmon Roe Pie

Makes 8 servings

1 small onion, minced
7 hard-boiled eggs, chopped
¼ teaspoon salt
¼ teaspoon pepper
1 tablespoon mayonnaise
1 pint sour cream
1 8-ounce package cream
  cheese at room
  temperature
  6-ounces salmon roe
  Crackers *or* dark bread
2 lemons, cut in wedges

Combine onion and chopped egg in a bowl. Add salt and pepper; stir in mayonnaise. Press mixture into a greased, deep, 10-inch pie plate; cover and chill overnight. Combine sour cream and cream cheese in small bowl; stir until smooth. Spoon over egg mixture; cover and chill for 2 hours. When ready to serve, carefully spoon caviar over top of pie. Serve with crackers or thinly sliced dark bread and lemon wedges.

Seafood Brochette

Makes 6 servings

½ cup dry white wine
4 tablespoons olive oil
2 cloves garlic, minced
4 tablespoons chopped
  parsley
  Salt and pepper to taste
½ teaspoon crumbled dried
  oregano
½ tablespoon crumbled
  dried basil
1½ pounds large scallops or
  salmon fillets, cut into
  1-inch pieces
1 pound large shrimp,
  shelled and deveined
1 pint cherry tomatoes
3 green peppers, cut into
  2-inch pieces
  Hot cooked rice

Combine wine, oil, garlic, and seasonings in a shallow glass dish; marinate scallops and shrimp for 4 hours, turning occasionally. Alternately thread scallops and shrimp with cherry tomatoes and green peppers, dividing between 6 skewers. Place skewers on a greased rack over hot grill or broil in oven. Cook for 8 minutes or until seafood is cooked, turning once and basting occasionally with marinade. Serve with hot rice.

Baked Potato Skins

Makes 6 servings

8 large potatoes, baked and
  cooled slightly
2 tablespoons butter, melted
½ pound bacon, fried,
  drained, and crumbled
6 green onions, minced
½ cup grated cheddar cheese

Preheat oven to 450°. Cut potatoes in half lengthwise; cut each half into thirds. Scoop out potatoes, leaving skin intact. Reserve pulp for another use. Sprinkle skins evenly with butter, bacon, and onions. Top with cheese; bake for 15 minutes or until crisp.

Creamed Spinach
Makes 6 servings

1 pound fresh spinach, trimmed, washed, and dried
4 tablespoons butter
3 tablespoons flour
½ pint heavy cream
Salt and pepper
¼ teaspoon wine vinegar
2 tablespoons butter, melted
3 tablespoons freshly grated Parmesan cheese

Preheat oven to 350°. Cook spinach in boiling salted water for 3 minutes; drain and set aside. Melt butter in a small saucepan; whisk in flour until absorbed. Stir in cream; simmer and whisk until sauce is desired thickness. Cool slightly; mix cream sauce into spinach. Add salt and pepper to taste; stir in vinegar and butter. Pour mixture into a 1½-quart casserole. Sprinkle with Parmesan cheese. Bake spinach for 10 minutes; stir immediately. This dish can be prepared ahead and refrigerated; reheat to serve.

Summer Squash
Makes 5 to 6 servings

4 small summer squash, thinly sliced
2 medium zucchini, thinly sliced
1 medium onion, thinly sliced
Salt
4 tablespoons butter at room temperature, cut into ½-inch pieces
Freshly ground pepper

Cook squash, zucchini, and onion in boiling salted water about 3-6 minutes, or until tender. Drain vegetables; toss with butter and pepper to taste. Serve hot.

Cherry Pie
Makes 6 servings

4 cups pitted tart cherries
1½ cups sugar
3 tablespoons tapioca
1 teaspoon lemon juice
½ teaspoon vanilla
Salt
2 tablespoons butter
2 9-inch pie crusts, unbaked

Preheat oven to 425°. Combine cherries, sugar, tapioca, lemon juice, vanilla, and salt to taste in a mixing bowl; set aside for ½ hour. Pour into pie crust; dot with butter. Cut remaining pie crust into strips; arrange in lattice-work style across top. Bake for 40 to 45 minutes. Cool on rack.